Old GOUROCK

by
Graham Twaddle

A horse and cart carrying farm produce, photographed at Ashton in 1879.

GOUROCK.

© Graham Twaddle 1999
First published in the United Kingdom, 1999,
by Stenlake Publishing
Telephone / Fax: 01290 551122

ISBN 1 84033 064 3

**The author's fee for writing this book has been donated to
the Ardgowan Hospice, Greenock.**

ACKNOWLEDGEMENTS

I am grateful to Malcolm Allan of the University of Strathclyde Library and to my father, Thomas Twaddle, for their assistance with this publication. I would also like to thank Oliver van Helden of Stenlake Publishing for suggesting the project in the first place.

The publishers would like to thank Robert Grieves for providing the pictures that appear on the back cover, the inside front cover, and pages 8, 12, 18, 20, 30, 33, 43 and 47.

THE PUBLISHERS REGRET THAT THEY CANNOT SUPPLY
COPIES OF ANY PICTURES FEATURED IN THIS BOOK.

From 1858 until the Scottish local government reorganisation of 1975, Gourock was a burgh, enjoying autonomy under its own town council. The old burgh coat of arms can now be seen on a few of the older buildings of Gourock, such as the Gamble Institute and the former municipal buildings. It is partly derived from the coat of arms of the Darroch family, who were the main land-owning family of the town. They made their fortune in the Caribbean, and the figure of a man at the top is said to represent the leader of a gang of slaves who stabbed himself in the chest upon capture.

BIBLIOGRAPHY

The Gourock Times
The Third Statistical Account of Scotland (1962)
Cormack, I. (1975) *Tramways of Greenock, Gourock and Port Glasgow*
MacArthur, I. (1971) *The Caledonian Steam Packet Co. Ltd.*
MacDougall, S. and Monteith, J. (1981) *Gourock, Inverkip and Wemyss Bay From Old Photographs*
Macrae, D. (1880) *Notes About Gourock*
Milne, C. (1958) *The Story of Gourock 1858 - 1958*
Snoddy, T. G. (1937) *Round about Greenock*

INTRODUCTION

The origin of the name Gourock is believed to come from the Gaelic for 'circular bay'. It is an apt name, for this natural harbour, 'very convenient for trade, having sufficient depth for vessels of any burden, and good shelter', has been at the core of Gourock's development as a town. In 1494 King James IV, sailing to the Western Isles, is said to have embarked at 'the Gouraik, on the west border and sea, aucht miles fra Dumberton or thereby'. The town is known to have once belonged to a branch of the Douglas family, whose castle stood in the grounds of what is now Darroch Park. When the family fell from royal favour, Gourock was ceded to Sir David Stewart of Castlemilk, and remained in the hands of the Stewart family for over three hundred years. In 1695 the village became a burgh of barony, which gave it the right to hold a weekly market.

Gourock was still little more than a small fishing village with less than 500 inhabitants when Sir John Stewart sold the estate for around £15,000 in 1784. The buyer was Duncan Darroch, a merchant who had returned to Scotland from the West Indies, and whose businessman's eye perhaps spotted the burgh's potential. During the late eighteenth and early nineteenth centuries fishing was the mainstay of the economy, but this was supplemented by the rise of small industries including a ropeworks, boatbuilders, quarry and a copper mine. Tourism too began to play its part in the town's livelihood: Gourock was discovered by the middle and upper classes of Glasgow as a sea-bathing resort, and wealthy city dwellers rented houses along the front during the summer months. According to one writer, commenting in 1842, 'the poor in this place have great advantages from the strangers who resort to it for sea-bathing quarters, who are very kind to them'. Nowadays it is hard to imagine the attraction, but prior to the coming of the railway and pier, Gourock Bay was described as 'a beautiful beach of white sand and pebbles'.

Up until the mid-nineteenth century the town developed predominantly along the eastern side of the bay, giving rise to the saying 'all to the one side – like Gourock'. But by the 1880s Gourock's population had more than tripled in size, and a long line of houses and development stretched along the coast and uphill as far as Ashton. The first main boost to Gourock's development came in 1858 when the newly appointed Burgh Council set about laying the foundations for future growth, installing mains water and sewerage within a few years. The other big influence was the coming of the railway. It reached Greenock in 1841 and for the first time brought Gourock within easy reach of the city. Even before the railway line to Gourock had opened in 1889, a regular tram service connecting Gourock and Greenock

made daily travel to Glasgow viable. Gourock became a desirable place to live, with attractive new villas for the professional classes growing up in its west end. It had joined the commuter belt.

As a busy railway terminus and steamer port Gourock prospered. As a Clyde holiday resort, it enjoyed a more modest success, but one that was sufficient to swell the population by almost half during the summer months. The highlight of the holiday season in the 1930s was the annual Gourock Carnival in July, a fortnight of sporting events and entertainment, culminating in a swimming competition across the Clyde from Gourock to Kilcreggan.

It was the outbreak of World War II that transformed this modest residential town and coastal resort into a place of national significance. In wartime, the long and heavily guarded entrance to the Clyde became a natural haven for shipping. Gourock's strategic position on the river made it the base for many important operations. Hotels and guest-houses in the town quickly filled up, and Gourock developed a cosmopolitan atmosphere, hosting Norwegian, Dutch, Polish, French and American military personnel, as well as servicemen and women from all over the country. One author goes so far as to say that 'During the Second World War, Gourock became one of the most important places in Britain'.

During the 1950s and 60s Gourock became less a resort, and more the dormitory town it is today, with a steady growth in population and the addition of some large new housing estates. The town's population now stands at around 11,743 inhabitants. Its dormitory status has not been without its effects on the social life of the town. Even as far back as the 1950s there was felt to be a 'lack in Gourock of that sense of community to be found in many other places of similar size'. A lack of local employment has also been a problem, and there are all too few local prospects for Gourockians these days.

The town itself appears shabbier in places than it does in the old photographs of this book, and the air of a small resort, even a faded one, has long gone. Among the older generation in particular, there are those who place much of the blame on Gourock's loss of its Burgh Council in the local government reorganisation of 1975, and its subsequent absorption into Inverclyde.

Surfing the Internet recently to see if there was anything about Gourock, I came across one intriguingly named site: 'Gourock: centre of the world'. Disappointingly, its author has yet to expand on this claim. The centre of the world it may not be, but even if it has seen better days, Gourock is still a pleasant place to live, with the continuing number of incomers and new housing developments testifying to the attractions of this corner of the Clyde.

The Pilot's Cottage, which survived until early this century, stood not far from the Cloch lighthouse. Its name recalls the days when the ferry to Cowal departed from nearby. This crossing was much in use up until the end of the eighteenth century and once formed part of an important route to the ancient kingdom of Dalriada in Argyll.

The Cloch Lighthouse sends a light across the firth to the Gantock Rocks. Built between 1795 and 1797, one of its designers was Robert Stevenson, grandfather of Robert Louis Stevenson. It once had a steam-powered foghorn, which was unpopular among residents who described it as sounding like 'a stupendous moan breaking into a sudden shriek'. During both world wars a boom was placed across the river from the lighthouse to prevent German vessels from entering and travelling up the firth. The view along this stretch of coastline is very fine: a promotional blurb from the 1960s mentions a claim that the walk from Gourock to the Cloch was 'the finest . . . in Scotland', and that 'the second finest was the walk back again!'. The lighthouse keepers' houses are now all private residences.

This building, at the site of the landing place of the old ferry to Cowal, was once the Ferry House and Inn and later became one of several temperance hotels in the area (although some temperance hotels were so-called more because they were unable to get a drinks license than because of their moral stance). An old drovers' road once passed through this spot: now there is a small industrial estate above this formerly unbroken stretch of greenbelt.

Levan Castle lay in ruins for over two centuries before being impressively restored as a domestic dwelling in the 1980s. It dates from the fifteenth and sixteenth centuries, and passed from the Morton family to Lord Semple in 1547 before becoming part of the Ardgowan Estate for many years. The nearby early nineteenth century mansion of Levanne House, once a hotel, is now being turned into flats. MacInroy's Point, where Western Ferries now operate a service to Cowal, takes its name from the family who built the house.

CLOCH ROAD LOOKING EAST, GOUROCK.   A.1238.

This picture dates from 1935 and shows some of the then very new bungalows that now extend right along Cloch Road. The bus in the picture was one of the fleet of William Dunlop, who operated the service between Greenock, Gourock and Largs.

Tinker's Well, Gourock.

Dated 1913, this picture shows the site of one of the main public wells in Gourock, which lay between Ashton Road and Cloch Road. It was supposedly named after a group of tinkers who camped there in 1826. The townspeople relied on these wells until the middle of the nineteenth century. There was no mains water supply in the town until April 1862.

 AERIAL VIEW, GOUROCK, SHOWING ROYAL YACHT CLUB HOUSE

This postcard, sent in 1922, shows the bottom end of Ashton Road, the yacht club, and above it the elegant Victorian and Edwardian villas of Victoria Road, Moorfield Road, and Ashgrove Avenue. Built on a steep hillside with only narrow access roads, these houses were better suited to the days before the motor car. For many years this end of town marked the boundary between the Burgh of Gourock and the neighbouring Ardgowan Estate, and the town expanded uphill rather than directly along the coast.

Yacht Club, Gourock.

Sailing has been a popular sport in Gourock for over a century. Founded in 1894, the Gourock Sailing Club received royal patronage in 1908, when it became the Royal Gourock Yacht Club. The clubhouse was built in 1903, a gift from the Paisley industrialist James Coats, who also donated the municipal chains of office in 1908. One of the highlights of the yachting year is in August when yachts attached to the club compete for the King George V Challenge Cup. This was presented to the club by the king when his yacht took part in the Clyde Yachting Regatta in 1920.

Trams first came to Gourock in 1873, when the Vale of Clyde Tramways Company built lines running from Greenock to Gourock along Cardwell Road, Shore Street, Kempock Street and Albert Road as far as Ashton. This picture was taken at the terminus at Ashton, roughly where the yacht club now stands. The first trams were horse-drawn and ran between the two towns every twenty minutes. An electrified service was introduced by the Greenock and Port Glasgow Tramways Company in 1901 and ran until July 1929 when the trams were scrapped in favour of buses. In spite of Gourock's wet climate, open-topped trams were the norm for many years.

The tenements to the left are those of Ashburn Gate and Ashburn Gardens, which were new when this postcard was sent in 1913. Unusually for the town, they are four rather than three stories high, reflecting the high demand for housing at the time, mainly due to an influx of families from Woolwich, London, who had come to work in the torpedo factory at Greenock. The view along Ashton Road looks very similar today.

In order to compete with other Clyde resorts Gourock needed a venue for indoor entertainment. Cragburn Pavilion on Albert Road was officially opened on 16 May 1936 with Sir Harry Lauder present. This picture shows it brand new in 1937. The pavilion was designed to be multi-purpose: it could be used for concerts, as a dance-hall, theatre, and occasionally as a cinema. In 1946 the town formally welcomed home its returning servicemen by hosting victory dinners there. Cragburn's heyday was between the 30s and early 1960s. Its Friday and Saturday night dances were the main attraction for young people at the time, and a trysting place for many a couple. As one lady recently put it: 'I thought the world would end if I didn't get to Cragburn every week!' Its life as a dance-hall ended in 1971, and after a period of neglect and under-use it was finally knocked down in the 1990s to be replaced by luxury flats.

As Gourock grew, houses along this part of the front became particularly sought after. An effusive visitor to the town in 1878 described it as 'one long line of architectural loveliness', adding, 'The houses are generally of the most tasteful design, with flower pots in front, and narrow patches of garden in the rear'. Severe winter weather frequently caused damage to this coast road, and in 1896 plans for esplanades and sea-walls along Gourock's east and west bays were drawn up. This part of the esplanade along Albert Road was completed in 1900.

Another view of the esplanade, *c.*1918. The fountain, which commemorates Queen Victoria's Diamond Jubilee of 1897, still stands, but has been relocated further along Albert Road. The girls with the parasols are obviously taking no chances with the Gourock weather.

A small turret and a crumbling wall, still visible today and once part of a mansion known as 'Bentley's Folly', can be seen to the far left of the tenements next to the children's pond in this picture. The house was described as having magnificent terraced gardens, battlements and goldfish ponds and was named after the English cotton merchant who had it built at great expense. Ruined by his extravagant lifestyle, he is said to have ended up in a Glasgow poorhouse. Built partly on land reclaimed from the sea, much of the house had fallen away by the late 1870s. The children's paddling ponds and sandpits look more appealing in the picture than they do today.

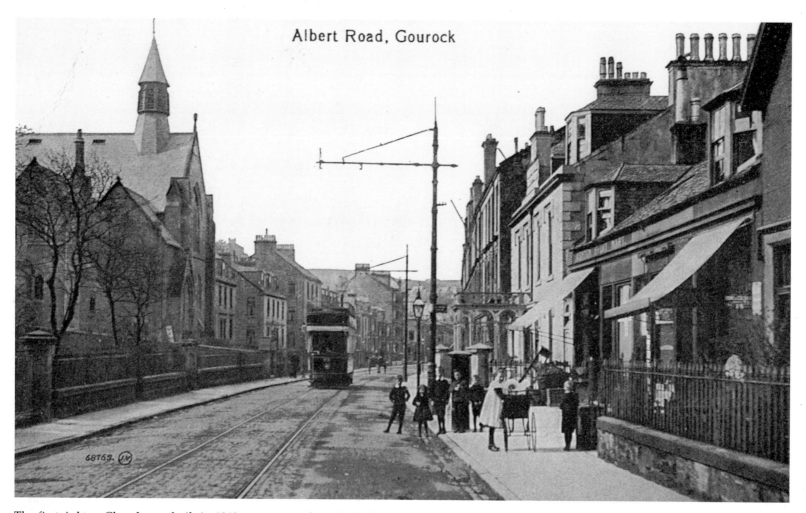

Albert Road, Gourock

The first Ashton Church was built in 1848 to accommodate Gourock's 'United Presbyterians' (the Presbyterian Church in Scotland being far from united at that time). When the belfry collapsed during a gale the building was declared unsafe and demolished. A second church (above) was built on the site, but was destroyed by fire in 1923. The third church and hall, dating from 1927, were closed and demolished in the 1980s and the site is now occupied by retirement flats. Rev. David Macrae, minister of the church between 1872 and 1879, was the author of several books including a history of Gourock. Expelled from his church in 1879 for his liberal views, he later became a Congregational minister in Dundee.

Ashton Road and Hotel, Gourock.

This postcard shows the Ashton Hotel, which stood in what is now Albert Road. The photograph dates from 1909, around which time a night at the Ashton would have cost 3 shillings. The hotel later changed its name to the Cloch and has since been demolished. New flats called Cloch Court now stand in its place.

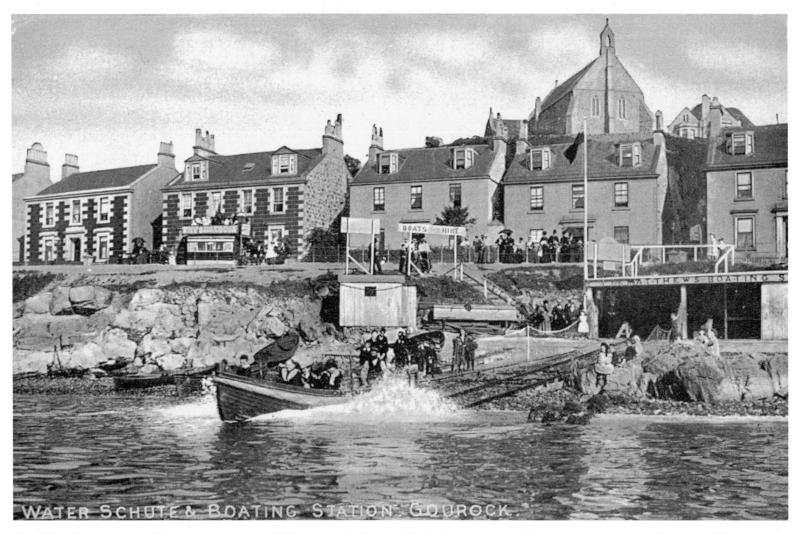

WATER SCHUTE & BOATING STATION, GOUROCK.

The Water Chute was a holiday attraction in the 1920s. In a ride that could only have lasted a few seconds, a boat was allowed to slide down the slipway at a speed fast enough to create the modest splash pictured. The passengers look fairly unruffled by the experience. The boating station can still be seen on Albert Road, but is now very run down, and you would be lucky to launch much from the slipway today.

Albert Road, showing the steps leading down to the boating station. In the days before purpose-built marinas, Gourock bay was popular as a mooring for yachts during the summer months, and there were several other slipways along this stretch of coast.

The west end of Gourock (above) has always been the more attractive end of the town; unfortunately for its credentials as a resort, city folk taking a trip 'doon the watter' would have arrived at the east end first. According to the Rev. Macrae, writing in 1880, 'Many people are repelled from Gourock by the prosaic aspect of the village as seen from the passing steamer, and still more by the unsightly appearance of the shore beside the pier with its litter of ugly sheds. The sight sends away many even of the poorer class . . .'. In reality, the lack of a decent beach at Gourock was probably a more important reason for resorts further down the coast being favoured.

Gourock was popular as a resort for sea-bathing as far back as the eighteenth century, and hot and cold sea-water baths were established just off Shore Street in 1844. In 1909 this swimming pool was opened at the far end of Kempock Street. It owes its current 30s-style decor to a major refit in 1935; this picture was taken around 1929, before the changing rooms and spectators' gallery were extended. Gourock's open-air pool is one of the last in Scotland, and although swimming is only available during the summer months a gym which is open all year round has recently been added. The sea-water pool was not heated until 1969, so the young bathers in the picture must have been hardy indeed.

The western end of Kempock Street at the beginning of the century. The drawbacks of horse-drawn trams may be seen from the manure in the street! Behind the tenements on the left was a shingle beach, which has now been built up as the town car park. The pump in the picture was once the main public water supply for this part of the town.

Kempock Street *c*.1910 showing overhead lines for electric trams. The shop with the awning on the right hand side was Ashton Library, one of the privately-owned circulating libraries which operated much like modern video rental shops.

The gable end to the left of this picture advertises the Ashton Cafe, which was run by the Giannini family for many years. It has now been replaced by modern flats. The war memorial was unveiled in 1922. There were civilian casualties too in Gourock as a result of air raids in October 1940 and May 1941; buildings on Shore Street and Cardwell Road were completely destroyed.

Kempock St. Gourock.

Kempock Street photographed *c*.1910, with Aikman's printing and stationery shop to the left. From 1908 to 1909 Mr Aikman ran a newspaper called the *Gourock Advertiser*. In 1912 his shop was taken over by J. & R. Simpson of Largs who relaunched the paper in 1915 as the *Gourock Times*, a weekly publication which then cost half a penny. Several generations of the Simpson family ran the paper until the last issue appeared in 1980. In spite of the introduction of electric trams, one of which can be seen in the background, some people at this time still travelled by horse-drawn vehicles such as the one at the extreme right hand side of the photograph.

To the left is Veitch's Temperance Hotel, later known as the Columba Temperance Hotel, and pulled down after a fire in the late 1950s. It was one of several hotels, including the Star and the Queen's, which were situated in this part of town and attracted business from the nearby railway and steamer terminals. In addition to running her hotel, Mrs Veitch also helped to found Gourock's Baptist Church in the 1890s.

Kempock Street a few years before the outbreak of World War I, showing two old Gourock establishments, the Kempock Bar and Cleat's Bar, both still in existence. In the 1880s there were 20 licensed premises in Gourock, a number which no doubt shocked the members of the Gourock Total Abstinence Society and the Gourock branch of the British Women's Temperance Association. In 1911 they went to the County Court complaining about Greenockians getting drunk in the town on days when the pubs in Greenock were closed.

The fountain at the entrance to Station Street was removed during World War II, when increased amounts of traffic made it a liability. It was gifted to the town by Captain Duncan McPherson, who in his will left provision for a small hospital to be built in Gourock. The McPherson Hospital was built at Midton and opened in 1925 with accommodation for 14 patients.

PIER HEAD, GOUROCK.

The row of shops with the awnings at the right hand side survived into the early 1980s. They were built at the turn of the century on the site of the old coastguard station. Among the businesses were Sharp's the watchmaker and jewellers, the Argyll Tearooms, McGlinchey the Pierhead barbers, Cannon's hardware store, and also on Station Road, Robertson's the photographers. In 1950 there were as many as 211 shops in Gourock. However, many of these relied on passing trade in the summer months, and had comparatively low turnovers. Inevitably, a large number have since closed down, and today most Gourockians do their shopping in Greenock or Glasgow.

Built in 1908, this hangar-like building was Gourock's main centre of indoor entertainment in the early part of the century. Known locally as the Kursaal (meaning 'a place of entertainment at a seaside resort'), it catered first for a roller-skating craze, but was later used as a jazz-dancing club (in the early 1920s), a cinema, for variety shows, and even for tennis and boxing matches. The building had fallen into disrepair by the early 1930s and was knocked down. 'Can you rink? – I can', wrote the sender of this card in 1909. 'It is fine fun, especially when you go on your head.'

A view of the Pierhead dating from 1936. The area to the left shows the site of the Kursaal, upon which the post office and the Bay Hotel were later built. On the right hand side of the picture can be seen MacKays Tearooms, now a Chinese restaurant, and beyond them the Old Glasgow pub and Gourock Picture House, now the site of Gourock library. The Picture House opened in 1914 and closed in the early 1960s after a very brief spell as a bingo hall. Among the many buses in the picture are, on the right, a Leyland double-decker belonging to Greenock Motor Services, who provided all the local transport in Greenock, Gourock and Port Glasgow at the time. The single deckers in the picture belonged to the Western SMT company, who operated services between Gourock and Glasgow. The gasholder in the distance belonged to the Gourock Gasworks Company, which was formed in 1848 to meet the town's lighting requirements.

The Pier, Gourock. Grk.88.

The station and pier c.1933. Little of the original Gourock station survives today, and the pier has fallen into such disrepair that much of it is now unsafe and closed to the public. In the 1940s the clock tower was removed to become a signalling tower. The pilot's office was located in the corner of the pier buildings and the small vessel moored nearby was one of the pilot cutters. Visible in the immediate foreground is the roof of a boathouse belonging to the Ritchie brothers, who for many years ran a small ferry between Gourock and Kilcreggan.

A wintry view of Gourock pier. The carts are laden with coal, destined to heat the boilers of the steamers which sailed from the town. Gourock was one of the main coaling stations for steamers, and it took about an hour to load a vessel's bunkers. Coal was transported to the awaiting steamer by horse and cart and unloaded by men known as 'the black squad'. After each refuelling, the ship's decks had to be hosed down to clean off the coal dust.

THE PIER, GOUROCK.

B.2051.

Gourock station and pier shortly after nationalisation in 1948. In 1957 some of the buildings were severely damaged by fire. Over the next few decades there was a marked decrease in river and rail traffic and by the 1970s much of this formerly grand Victorian station and pier had fallen into disrepair. Today the only regular sailings from the pier are the Caledonian MacBrayne car ferry to Dunoon, and a small ferry service to Kilcreggan and Helensburgh.

PIERHEAD AND BAY HOTEL, GOUROCK

B 2045

The Pierhead as it appeared in the 1950s. Half a century later, few of the original buildings remain. To the right of the Bay Hotel is the post office which was opened in 1938 and demolished in February 1999. What will replace it remains to be seen.

The Bay Hotel opened on 12 April 1938 and was built to accommodate visitors to the Glasgow Empire Exhibition of that year. At the time it was the height of modernity and elegance, boasting not only hot and cold running water in its 37 bedrooms, but also cocktail bars, an elevator and a roof garden. A year later it was hosting child survivors from torpedoed ships. The Bay was at its busiest during the war, when Gourock's strategic position made the town a centre of activity. In later years the hotel went into decline, hosted a disco, and lent a generally shabby image to Gourock town centre. It is shortly to be demolished and will no doubt take a few tales with it.

The "Castle", Gourock.

Hardly a trace of Gourock's original castle remains – the stronghold, built in the 1400s by the Douglas family, was demolished in the eighteenth century and its site lies within the Darroch Park. The 'Castle' pictured here was in fact a private house, built in 1840 for the captain of a Belfast steamer. It was later occupied by a Mr Zoller, the Belgian consul in Glasgow, who is said to have flown his national flag from one of its towers. The Castle was put up for sale in 1896 and in spite of a general feeling that it should be purchased by the town council, fell to a building syndicate who promptly knocked it down. Nothing of it remains today except for an extremely weathered white marble plaque inscribed in German, in memory of Mr Zoller, which lies just behind the Granny Kempock stone.

BOWLING GREEN, GOUROCK HOUSE, GOUROCK.

207108. J.V.

NO DOGS ADMITTED

A game of bowls on a summer's day, still a common site on Barrhill Road. Gourock Bowling Club was founded in 1866, and during World War II one of the greens was used as a temporary camp for American servicemen; prior to that potatoes had been grown on it as part of the war effort. The tenements in the background are Castle Mansions and Castle Gardens, so-named because they were built on the site of Gourock 'Castle'. To the right is St John's Church, built to accommodate those Gourockians, including the parish minister and laird, who had broken away from the Established Church at the Great Disruption in 1843. It was opened in 1857. The site of its once grand manse is now the St John's Manor flats on Barrhill Road.

St Bartholomew's Episcopal Church was built in 1857 at a cost of £700, a sum raised largely by donations. Its congregation was at its greatest after a large number of torpedo factory workers from Woolwich settled in the area in 1913. Gourock's First Company of the Boys' Brigade was founded at the church in 1892. At the corner of Barrhill Road and Binnie Street stands Marymount, a house once used as a convent, and which together with the St John's manse next door was taken over by the Admiralty during the war. The fine wrought-iron railings of the house on the corner were, like so many others, removed during World War II for scrap metal as part of the war effort.

THE GLEN, GOUROCK.

The Glen, as it is popularly called, lies between the late Victorian villas of Victoria Road and a newer housing estate along Divert Road. It is the site of a small waterfall, created by the Ash Burn as it trickles down the hillside towards Ashton Bay. Pre-war maps of Gourock show this side of the town to have been fields and farmland, and the names of old farms – Divert, Drumshantie, Trumpethill and Midton – still survive in street and housing estate names. The bridge no longer stands, and the Glen is now a sorry mess of empty bottles and cans.

This picture was taken on one of the slopes of Tower Hill, just above Broomberry Drive. The top of the hill, originally called Barr Hill, is the highest point in the town; the tower which crowns it was built in the mid-nineteenth century by General Darroch, the Laird of Gourock. In Victorian times one of Gourock's main exports was whinstone, and a section of the hill was the site of a quarry. Much of the stone used to pave the streets of Greenock, Paisley and Glasgow was quarried from Gourock at Craigmushat (meaning 'beautiful rock'), which left a gouge in the hillside that was anything but beautiful. It is now, controversially, a land-fill site. Tower Hill was acquired by the town in 1945 and is a rather untended piece of public parkland today. To the left of the photograph is the square tower of Old Gourock Parish Church, completed in 1832. Gourock formerly belonged to the Parish of Inverkip, and up until 1776 locals had to walk there on Sundays for church.

The closest thing Gourock has to a town hall is the Gamble Institute, donated to the town in 1874 by Mrs Henry Gamble in memory of her husband. It originally comprised two halls, a coffee and smoking room, bathrooms, a library and later a billiard room. The institute was intended primarily for working men, and it was the philanthropic aim of its governing committee that it should 'attract them away from the dangerous fascinations of vice in its various forms, and improve them morally, intellectually and physically'. The Gamble Institute passed to the council in 1916 and has a less ambitious remit nowadays. On the left hand side of the street can be seen the steps of the Gamble Bridge, which used to lead to the east end of Gourock pier.

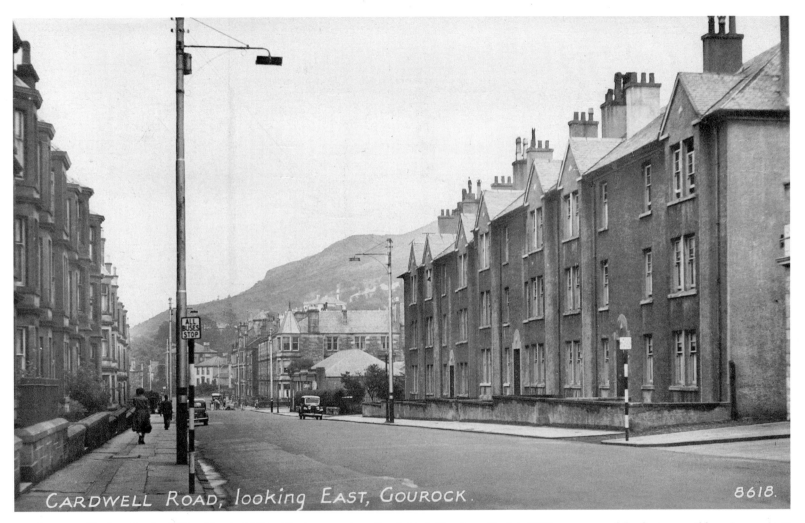

CARDWELL ROAD, looking EAST, GOUROCK.

8618.

An almost traffic-free Cardwell Road in the 1950s. The tenement on the right, dating from the late 1920s, was one of the first council housing projects in Gourock. The Western SMT bus depot stood next door.

COVE ROAD, CARDWELL BAY, GOUROCK

A.8685

Cove Road is the home of Gourock's other sailing club, Cardwell Bay Sailing Club, founded in 1906. This part of the esplanade was completed in 1899. Many of the small industries that grew up in Gourock, mainly concerned with boats, were situated here. The world famous Gourock Ropeworks was founded behind Cove Road in 1737, but later moved to Port Glasgow, and Cove Road was also the site of a small sail-making firm and two boatbuilders.

This view of Gourock Bay from the eastern esplanade illustrates the length of the pier and station buildings. To the right of the picture is a luxury steam yacht. Among the private yachts to anchor here were Sir Thomas Lipton's *Shamrock*, King George V's *Britannia*, and even the yacht belonging to the German Kaiser. Before the pier was built, ships berthed at a small quay situated just off Hopeton Street, near where the post office and the Bay Hotel were later built. It was there, in 1688, that the first red herring in Britain is said to have been cured, by a Glasgow magistrate. To date this is Gourock's only claim to culinary fame.

Although this postcard is captioned HM Torpedo Factory, Gourock, the factory actually lay just across the town's boundary in Greenock. It opened in 1911, having been transferred from Woolwich, and brought 700 staff and their families into the area. A deputation of workers were unimpressed by the standard of housing on offer in Greenock, commenting that they 'were not desirous of living and sleeping in one apartment, and that a hole in the wall for a bed was objectionable'. As a result, many of the Woolwichers subsequently chose to settle in Gourock, and the town's population increased by around 2,000 at the time. The factory was transferred to Alexandria at the end of the war and closed completely in 1960.